BEST-LOVED
OSCAR
WILDE

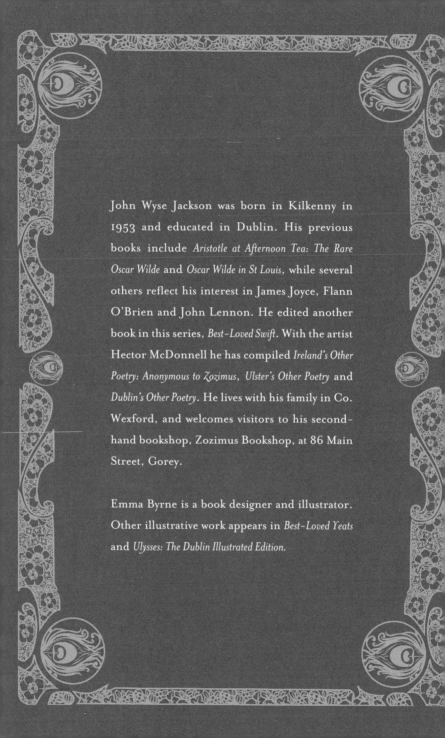

John Wyse Jackson was born in Kilkenny in 1953 and educated in Dublin. His previous books include *Aristotle at Afternoon Tea: The Rare Oscar Wilde* and *Oscar Wilde in St Louis*, while several others reflect his interest in James Joyce, Flann O'Brien and John Lennon. He edited another book in this series, *Best-Loved Swift*. With the artist Hector McDonnell he has compiled *Ireland's Other Poetry: Anonymous to Zozimus*, *Ulster's Other Poetry* and *Dublin's Other Poetry*. He lives with his family in Co. Wexford, and welcomes visitors to his second-hand bookshop, Zozimus Bookshop, at 86 Main Street, Gorey.

Emma Byrne is a book designer and illustrator. Other illustrative work appears in *Best-Loved Yeats* and *Ulysses: The Dublin Illustrated Edition*.

EDITED BY
JOHN WYSE
JACKSON

BEST·LOVED

OSCAR
WILDE

ILLUSTRATIONS BY EMMA BYRNE

PB

THE O'BRIEN PRESS
DUBLIN

First published 2015 by The O'Brien Press Ltd.
12 Terenure Road East, Rathgar, Dublin 6, D06 HD27, Ireland.
Tel: +353 1 4923333; Fax: +353 1 4922777
E-mail: books@obrien.ie; Website: www.obrien.ie
Reprinted 2018.
The O'Brien Press is a member of Publishing Ireland.

ISBN: 978-1-78849-077-1

10 9 8 7 6 5 4 3 2
23 22 21 20 19 18

Cover illustration: Emma Byrne
Editing, typesetting, layout and design: The O'Brien Press Ltd
Printed and bound in the Czech Republic by Finidr Ltd.
The paper in this book is produced using pulp from managed forests.

Published in:

DUBLIN

UNESCO
City of Literature

In happy and loving memory of Ruth Ellen Moller

CONTENTS

IN FULL PURSUIT

PLAYWRIGHT, SOCIAL COMMENTATOR AND WIT

THE LOVE THAT DARE NOT SPEAK ITS NAME

SCANDAL AND IMPRISONMENT

THE CRYSTAL OF A POET'S HEART

POEMS AND ENDINGS

INTRODUCTION

'The two great turning points in my life were when my father sent me to Oxford, and when society sent me to prison.'

If your father is the country's most famous medical man, an eminent natural historian, antiquarian and serial adulterer, and if your mother is a revolutionary poet, Irish folklorist and literary hostess of legendary eccentricity, and if they name you Oscar Fingal O'Flahertie Wills Wilde, you have a lot to live up to.

Oscar was born in Dublin, at 21 Westland Row, on 16 October 1854. After boarding school in Enniskillen, he studied classics at Trinity College, Dublin, and then went (with a scholarship) to Magdalen College, Oxford. There he allied himself with the 'Aesthetes,' imbibing the 'gospel of beauty' from Walter Pater and the great John Ruskin, and travelling in Greece and Italy during vacations.

He moved in 1879 to London, where his name was soon being heard in literary, artistic and theatrical circles –

though less on account of his first book, *Poems* (1881), than for his flamboyant conversation. The year 1882 was spent in America and Canada, delivering provocative lectures about Aestheticism and the new British movement in art. (The following year was largely taken up with touring the British Isles, lecturing about the Americans and their lack of Aestheticism.) Wilde was now one of the most famous cultural figures in the world, even though, in truth, he had as yet published very little of real substance.

In 1884 he married Constance Lloyd, and they had two children, Cyril and Vyvyan. Still without regular means of support, he enjoyed himself for a time editing the *Woman's World* magazine and writing reviews. Between 1888 and 1895 were his most productive and successful years: he wrote short stories, essays, poems long and short, fairy tales, a shocking novel and five plays, each more accomplished than the last. In these works, and in interviews, letters and talks, his detached, teasing opinions challenged the absurdities and injustices of life in England in the late Victorian period.

If the rise of Oscar's star was rapid, its fall was meteoric. Acts of homosexuality were against not only the law of the land but the unwritten laws of society as well, and he showed exceptional courage in asserting publicly that same-sex love was a natural part of human life. His love for Lord Alfred ('Bosie') Douglas led to imprisonment with hard labour for two years. Released in 1897, he never recovered from the experience and died in Paris, three years later, aged forty-six.

Oscar once remarked: 'I put all my genius into my life; I put only my talent into my works.' Nothing could be further from the truth. Yes, the course of his life was a tragedy of Greek (or Shakespearian) proportions, a classic tale of success and failure, pride and prejudice. Following his death, this tale was told repeatedly, in books, in films and, naturally, in gossip. His literary achievement was underestimated, however, and his works were neglected by academic scholarship until the 1980s. Conversely, the popularity of his fiction, fairy tales and plays never waned.

Perhaps it was his Irishness that enabled Wilde to diagnose the hypocrisies of the English society in which he lived. He questioned everything, took nothing for granted. Once had found his voice, he found writing easy. The selection here is not limited to extracts from his most famous works; there are examples from many (though not all) of the literary forms he mastered. This book aims to show why Oscar Wilde is truly one of the 'best loved' writers, not just of Ireland, but of the world.

John Wyse Jackson

From THE PICTURE OF DORIAN GRAY

The Picture of Dorian Gray is a moral tale, revealing the horrors of a life
lived entirely for pleasure; and, since it describes these horrors
in glorious detail, it not only scandalised reviewers but also sold
in great numbers. The first version of *Dorian Gray* appeared in
Lippincott's Magazine in July 1890. For its publication in book form,
a year later, Wilde added six new chapters and, to explain the
philosophical underpinning of the book, a preface consisting
entirely of paradoxes. Wilde's aphorisms remain among his most
famous accomplishments today. Originally bearing the draft title
'Dogmas for the Use of the Aged', they offer a witty summary of
Aestheticism, the artistic creed that lies behind many of Wilde's
writings.

To reveal art and conceal the artist is art's aim.

The critic is he who can translate into another manner or a new material his impression of beautiful things.

The highest, as the lowest, form of criticism is a mode of autobiography.

Those who find ugly meanings in beautiful things are corrupt without being charming. This is a fault.

Those who find beautiful meanings in beautiful things are the cultivated. For these there is hope.

They are the elect to whom beautiful things mean only Beauty.

There is no such thing as a moral or an immoral book. Books are well written, or badly written. That is all.

The nineteenth century dislike of Realism is the rage of Caliban seeing his own face in a glass.

The nineteenth century dislike of Romanticism is the rage of Caliban not seeing his own face in a glass.

The moral life of man forms part of the subject-matter of the artist, but the morality of art consists in the perfect use of an imperfect medium. No artist desires to prove anything. Even things that are true can be proved.

No artist has ethical sympathies. An ethical sympathy in an artist is an unpardonable mannerism of style.

No artist is ever morbid. The artist can express everything.

Thought and language are to the artist instruments of an art.

Vice and virtue are to the artist materials for an art.

From the point of view of form, the type of all the arts is the art of the musician. From the point of view of feeling, the actor's craft is the type.

All art is at once surface and symbol.

Those who go beneath the surface do so at their peril.

Those who read the symbol do so at their peril.

It is the spectator, and not life, that art really mirrors.

Diversity of opinion about a work of art shows that the work is new, complex, and vital.

When critics disagree the artist is in accord with himself.

We can forgive a man for making a useful thing as long as he does not admire it. The only excuse for making a useless thing is that one admires it intensely.

All art is quite useless.

HÉLAS!

In 1881, long before the daring accomplishments of *Dorian Gray*, Wilde's first book appeared. It did not sell particularly well. Simply called *Poems*, it offered a rich blend of imagery and ideas, elements often derived from the poets Wilde worshipped: Shakespeare, Donne, Swinburne, Byron, Keats and others. 'This is a volume of echoes, it is Swinburne and water', wrote *Punch* magazine, but the book's best poems have proved their durability — today they are probably better loved than any of Swinburne's. Initially, Wilde planned to open the volume with a remark made by John Keats: 'I have not the slightest feeling of humility towards the public or to anything in existence but the Eternal being, the Principle of Beauty, and the Memory of great men.' Perhaps wisely, before publication he replaced this quotation with this poem, written while he was still up at Oxford. 'Hélas!' ('Alas!') explores a dilemma that would follow its writer through life. (The last two lines are an adaptation of a biblical idea, from I Samuel 14:43.)

To drift with every passion till my soul
Is a stringed lute on which all winds can play,
Is it for this that I have given away
Mine ancient wisdom, and austere control?
Methinks my life is a twice-written scroll
Scrawled over on some boyish holiday
With idle songs for pipe and virelay
Which do but mar the secret of the whole.
Surely there was a time I might have trod
The sunlit heights, and from life's dissonance
Struck one clear chord to reach the ears of God:
Is that time dead? lo! with a little rod
I did but touch the honey of romance—
And must I lose a soul's inheritance?

REQUIESCAT

In 1867, when Wilde was twelve, his younger sister Isola died after a fever. He was very deeply affected and spent many hours alone by her grave in St John's Graveyard, Edgeworthstown, Co. Longford. At nineteen, on a visit to Avignon, he remembered her in this poem. The lines evoke the Elizabethan madrigal, with a melodious restraint not unlike the early verses of James Joyce (written in Dublin over two decades later). Deceptively simple, 'Requiescat' ('May She Rest') confronts the reality of death, moving from a fond sense of Isola's presence in the first verse to the final realisation that she has irrevocably gone from him. All his life Wilde carefully preserved a twist of Isola's hair – after his own death it was found in his hotel room in Paris.

Tread lightly, she is near
   Under the snow,
Speak gently, she can hear
   The daisies grow.

All her bright golden hair
   Tarnished with rust,
She that was young and fair
   Fallen to dust.

Lily-like, white as snow,
   She hardly knew
She was a woman, so
   Sweetly she grew.

Coffin-board, heavy stone,
   Lie on her breast,
I vex my heart alone
   She is at rest.

Peace, Peace, she cannot hear
   Lyre or sonnet,
All my life's buried here,
   Heap earth upon it.

ON IRISH HOME RULE

In 1882, Wilde discovered America. Richard D'Oyly Carte, producer of *Patience*, Gilbert and Sullivan's light operatic satire on the Aesthetes, had invited him there to explain Aestheticism, so that audiences in New York might appreciate the show's humour. The assignment developed into a lecture tour lasting almost a year. It was in the city of St Louis, Missouri (where much of the population had Irish blood) that Wilde most clearly expressed his advanced views on the struggles of the Irish people against landlordism and on Charles Stewart Parnell's policy of Home Rule. He never forgot that his mother was Speranza, the poet whose incendiary writings had ignited the Young Irelanders into rebellion in 1848: despite spending almost half his life in England, he would always remain an advocate of self-government for his native land. Once, while rowing with others on the Thames, when a political disagreement arose about Home Rule,

Wilde calmed it with the words, 'Ah! My own idea is that Ireland should rule England.'

'What are your feelings with regard to the Land League?' queried a GLOBE-DEMOCRAT reporter of Oscar Wilde last evening.

The 'aesthete' was sipping a glass of Apollinaris and smoking a cigarette. He promptly replied:

'As regards the general principle, that the only basis of legislation should be the general welfare of the people – and that is the only test by which the right of any citizen to hold property or possess any privileges should be viewed – I am entirely at one with the position held by the Land League,' replied Mr. Wilde. He continued: 'The land of Ireland, like the land of England, is perfectly unfairly divided, and the peasantry of Ireland have never had the proper conditions necessary for any real civilization at all. They have lived in the most impoverished way, in a certain state of life in which the only opening for any improvement was for them to leave their own country.'

'In this connection,' interrupted the reporter, 'do you believe in the wholesale emigration of the Irish from their native land?'

The question was scarcely asked when Mr. Wilde replied, 'I shall always hope that there shall be some people left in Ireland.' After thinking a while, he said, 'With regard to emigration from Ireland, it has had a great deal of influence in one way – in the way of reactions from America, not merely in people returning from America, a people bringing with them money to an impoverished country, but in a reaction of American thought on Irish politics. This modern public spirit with Irish politics is an entirely new departure in the history of Ireland; it is due entirely to the reflex influence of American politics.'

The Aesthete here lit a cigarette, and continued:

'With regard to the Land Bill, the mistake which I think the English Government are making is in thinking that they can permanently benefit one class in a community by permanently impoverishing the other. Up to this the gentry of Ireland have been rich and the peasant poor. They have merely transferred the burden from the peasant to the educated classes. They have not really alleviated the poverty of Ireland. They have merely removed its position and in one single act of legislation have swept away a great deal of the best civilization in Ireland. What I would wish to see would be the Government purchasing the land of Ireland from the landlords at a fair rate, giving them compensation as they gave the members of the Irish Church, and distributing that land amongst the people, issuing State bonds on which the people would pay an interest. This was the method adopted in Prussia, and it has there been in the highest degree beneficial.'

'What do you think of the "no-rent manifesto"?' asked the reporter.

'It is the one foolish thing that the Land League have done,' replied Mr. Wilde.

'Why so?'

'Because,' replied he, 'it strikes at the root of all civilization, of all fair dealing and of all common sense.'

The 'no-rent manifesto' having been explained to Mr. Wilde, the latter replied,

'You must remember that a manifesto of that kind, beside the mere words of it, there is always a latent spirit in it which is always understood to mean more than it expresses. In Ireland it was understood to be absolutely "No rent," which, however, I have no doubt that the most thoughtful amongst the Land League would not approve of.'

'You know Parnell, Sullivan, McCarthy and other members of the Land League?'

'I do,' he replied.

'Do you think that they would advocate anything unreasonable or nonsensical?'

'It is no compliment to generalise about a man,' answered Mr. Wilde. 'With regard to any agitation of this kind it is entirely a question of result. The means of every revolution are justified only by one thing – by the success of that revolution. A compulsory sale and fair compensation clause seems to me to be the remedy for the present evil system of land tenure in Ireland.'

'It is easy,' he added, 'for one to point out in revolutions great excesses, even great crimes. No measure probably ever produced so much immediate suffering and immediate crime as the French Revolution, and no measure was ever productive of so much good afterwards. It is very easy to object to the means of a revolution, to lay one's finger on certain excesses; the only way to judge of an agitation is by the success. In a political party it is not a question of whether they were wise or fair; the only way we can tell if they are wise is by their success.'

'Their measures are unwise if they do not succeed?'

'Certainly. Politics is a practical science. An unsuccessful revolution is merely treason; a successful one is a great era in the history of a country.'

'Are you in favour of the total separation of Ireland from the United Kingdom?'

'There is another folly,' replied Mr. Wilde. 'It is only a question of whether a country is able to assert its independence. At present I think it would be unwise in Ireland to claim total separation, because I do not think she would be able to preserve it, and to attempt anything that one cannot do is the only crime in politics. The first step to do should be a local Parliament, which I sincerely hope they will get, and it is an issue which my father was one of the first men in Ireland to advocate.'

'Then,' said the reporter, 'I may put you down as a Home Ruler?'

'You may,' he emphatically replied.

From *IMPRESSIONS OF AMERICA*

When he returned from his tour of the New World, Wilde was more famous than anyone could have imagined. He had, however, managed to save very little from his earnings, and soon was travelling around Great Britain and Ireland with a second series of talks. This time he not only spoke on art and Aestheticism but also entertained audiences with lively accounts of his experiences in America.

From Salt Lake City one travels over the great plains of Colorado and up the Rocky Mountains, on the top of which is Leadville, the richest city in the world. It has also got the reputation of being the roughest, and every man carries a revolver. I was told that if I went there they would be sure to shoot me or my travelling manager. I wrote and told them that nothing that they could do to my travelling manager would intimidate me.

They are miners — men working in metals, so I lectured to them on the Ethics of Art. I read them passages from the autobiography of Benvenuto Cellini and they seemed much delighted. I was reproved by my hearers for not having brought him with me. I explained that he had been dead for some little time which elicited the enquiry 'Who shot him?' They afterwards took me to a dancing saloon where I saw the only rational method of art criticism I have ever come across. Over the piano was printed a notice:—

PLEASE DO NOT SHOOT THE PIANIST.
HE IS DOING HIS BEST.

The mortality among pianists in that place is marvellous. Then they asked me to supper, and having accepted, I had to descend a mine in a rickety bucket in which it was impossible to be graceful. Having got into the heart of the mountain I had supper, the first course being whisky, the second whisky and the third whisky.

I went to the Theatre to lecture and I was informed that just before I went there two men had been seized for committing a murder, and in that theatre they had been brought on to the stage at eight o'clock in the evening, and then and there tried and executed before a crowded audience.

But I found these miners very charming and not at all rough.

Among the more elderly inhabitants of the South I found a melancholy tendency to date every event of importance by the late war. 'How beautiful the moon is to-night,' I once remarked to a gentleman who was standing next to me. 'Yes,' was his reply, 'but you should have seen it before the war.'

So infinitesimal did I find the knowledge of Art, west of the Rocky Mountains, that an art patron — one who in his day had been a miner — actually sued the railroad company for damages because the plaster cast of Venus of Milo, which he had imported from Paris, had been delivered minus the arms. And, what is more surprising still, he gained his case and the damages.

A CHANGE IN THE WEATHER
FATHER AND STORYTELLER

TO MY WIFE
WITH A COPY OF MY POEMS

In November 1883, Wilde lectured in Dublin, where an eighteen-year-old poet called Willie Yeats heard him. So too did a young art student, Constance Lloyd, with whom Wilde had fallen in love. He visited Constance the next day at her Dublin home and proposed to her in the ancestral drawing room. He was promptly accepted. They were married in London in May. Wilde designed the 'rich creamy satin' wedding dress, tinted delicately in 'cowslip'.

The groom inscribed these gentle lines in Constance's copy of his *Poems*. To call your new wife a 'poem' and to imagine a sheet of your verses settling on her hair might invite ridicule today, but such notions were then quite pardonable in London Aesthetic circles. The poem testifies to Wilde's faith in Constance's understanding of him, whatever the future might bring.

I can write no stately proem
    As a prelude to my lay;
From a poet to a poem
    I would dare to say.

For if of these fallen petals
    One to you seem fair,
Love will waft it till it settles
    On your hair.

And when wind and winter harden
    All the loveless land,
It will whisper of the garden,
    You will understand.

From 'THE SELFISH GIANT'

The couple were blessed with two adored children, Cyril and Vyvyan. Wilde was an attentive father and enjoyed romping around the dining room on all fours with the lads. At bedtime he would sing songs to them in Irish or tell them simplified versions of his fairy tales. In later life, Vyvyan recalled that his father had tears in his eyes when he told them the story of the Selfish Giant. When he asked him why, Wilde said that really beautiful things always made him cry.

*E*very afternoon, as they were coming from school, the children used to go and play in the Giant's garden.

It was a large lovely garden, with soft green grass. Here and there over the grass stood beautiful flowers like stars, and there were twelve peach-trees that in the spring-time broke out into delicate blossoms of pink and pearl, and in the autumn bore rich fruit. The birds sat on the trees and sang so sweetly that the children used to stop their games in order to listen to them. 'How happy we are here!' they cried to each other.

One day the Giant came back. He had been to visit his friend the Cornish ogre, and had stayed with him for seven years. After the seven years were over he had said all that he had to say, for his conversation was limited, and he determined to return to his own castle. When he arrived he saw the children playing in the garden.

'What are you doing there?' he cried in a very gruff voice, and the children ran away.

'My own garden is my own garden,' said the Giant; 'any one can understand that, and I will allow nobody to play in it but myself.' So he built a high wall all round it, and put up a notice-board.

TRESPASSERS
WILL BE
PROSECUTED

He was a very selfish Giant.

The poor children had now nowhere to play. They tried to play on the road, but the road was very dusty and full of hard stones, and they did not like it. They used to wander round the high wall when their lessons were over, and talk about the beautiful garden inside. 'How happy we were there,' they said to each other.

Then the Spring came, and all over the country there were little blossoms and little birds. Only in the garden of the Selfish Giant it was still winter. The birds did not care to sing in it as there were no children, and the trees forgot to blossom. Once a beautiful flower put its head out from the grass, but when it saw the notice-board it was so sorry for the children that it slipped back into the ground again, and went off to sleep. The only people who were pleased were the Snow and the Frost. 'Spring has forgotten this garden,' they cried, 'so we will live here all the year round.' The Snow covered up the grass with her great white cloak, and the Frost painted all the trees silver. Then they invited the North Wind to stay with them, and he came. He was wrapped in furs, and he roared all day about the garden, and blew the chimney-pots down. 'This is a delightful spot,' he said, 'we must ask the Hail on a visit.' So the Hail came. Every day for three hours he rattled on the roof of the castle till he broke most of the slates, and then he ran round and round the garden as fast as he could go. He was dressed in grey, and his breath was like ice.

'I cannot understand why the Spring is so late in coming,' said the Selfish Giant, as he sat at the window and looked out at his cold, white garden; 'I hope there will be a change in the weather.'

But the Spring never came, nor the Summer. The Autumn gave golden fruit to every garden, but to the Giant's garden she gave none. 'He is too selfish,' she said. So it was always Winter there, and the North Wind and the Hail, and the Frost, and the Snow danced about through the trees.

One morning the Giant was lying awake in bed when he heard some lovely music. It sounded so sweet to his ears that he thought it must be the King's musicians passing by. It was really only a little linnet singing outside his window, but it was so long since he had heard a bird sing in his garden that it seemed to him to be the most beautiful music in the world. Then the Hail stopped dancing over his head, and the North Wind ceased roaring, and a delicious perfume came to him through the open casement. 'I believe the Spring has come at last,' said the Giant; and he jumped out of bed and looked out.

What did he see?

He saw a most wonderful sight. Through a little hole in the wall the children had crept in, and they were sitting in the branches of the trees. In every tree that he could see there was a little child. And the trees were so glad to have the children back again that they had covered themselves with blossoms, and were waving their arms gently above the children's heads. The birds were flying about and twittering with delight, and the flowers were looking up through the green grass and laughing. It was a lovely scene, only in one corner it was still winter. It was the farthest corner of the garden, and in it was standing a little boy. He was so small that he could not reach up to the branches of the tree, and he was wandering all round it, crying bitterly. The poor tree was still quite covered with frost and snow, and the North Wind was blowing and roaring above it. 'Climb up! little boy,' said the Tree, and it bent its branches down as low as it could; but the boy was too tiny.

And the Giant's heart melted as he looked out. 'How selfish I have been!' he said; 'now I know why the Spring would not come here. I will put that poor little boy on the top of the tree, and then I will knock down the wall, and my garden shall be the children's playground for ever and ever.' He was really very sorry for what he had done.

So he crept downstairs and opened the front door quite softly, and went out into the garden. But when the children saw him they were so frightened that they all ran away, and the garden became winter again. Only the little boy did not run, for his eyes were so full of tears that he did not see the Giant coming. And the Giant stole up behind him and took him gently in his hand, and put him up into the tree. And the tree broke at once into blossom, and the birds came and sang on it, and the little boy stretched out his two arms and flung them round the Giant's neck, and kissed him. And the other children, when they saw that the Giant was not wicked any longer, came running back, and with them came the Spring. 'It is your garden now, little children,' said the Giant, and he took a great axe and knocked down the wall. And when the people were going to market at twelve o'clock they found the Giant playing with the children in the most beautiful garden they had ever seen.

All day long they played, and in the evening they came to the Giant to bid him good-bye.

'But where is your little companion?' he said: 'the boy

I put into the tree.' The Giant loved him the best because he had kissed him.

'We don't know,' answered the children; 'he has gone away.'

'You must tell him to be sure and come here to-morrow,' said the Giant. But the children said that they did not know where he lived, and had never seen him before; and the Giant felt very sad.

Every afternoon, when school was over, the children came and played with the Giant. But the little boy whom the Giant loved was never seen again. The Giant was very kind to all the children, yet he longed for his first little friend, and often spoke of him. 'How I would like to see him!' he used to say.

Years went over, and the Giant grew very old and feeble. He could not play about any more, so he sat in a huge arm-chair, and watched the children at their games, and admired his garden. 'I have many beautiful flowers,' he said; 'but the children are the most beautiful flowers of all.'

One winter morning he looked out of his window as he was dressing. He did not hate the Winter now, for he knew that it was merely the Spring asleep, and that the flowers were resting.

Suddenly he rubbed his eyes in wonder and looked and looked. It certainly was a marvellous sight. In the farthest corner of the garden was a tree quite covered with lovely white blossoms. Its branches were golden, and silver fruit hung down from them, and underneath it stood the little boy he had loved.

Downstairs ran the Giant in great joy, and out into the garden. He hastened across the grass, and came near to the child. And when he came quite close his face grew red with anger, and he said, 'Who hath dared to wound thee?' For on the palms of the child's hands were the prints of two nails, and the prints of two nails were on the little feet.

'Who hath dared to wound thee?' cried the Giant; 'tell me, that I may take my big sword and slay him.'

'Nay!' answered the child: 'but these are the wounds of Love.'

'Who art thou?' said the Giant, and a strange awe fell on him, and he knelt before the little child.

And the child smiled on the Giant, and said to him, 'You let me play once in your garden, to-day you shall come with me to my garden, which is Paradise.'

And when the children ran in that afternoon, they found the Giant lying dead under the tree, all covered with white blossoms.

AUNT JANE'S BALL

Throughout his life, Wilde told stories not just to children but to friends and acquaintances as well. When he came to dinner, the hosts would insist that he could not leave before relating one of his tales. Only a few of these were ever written down. Wilde seems to have based this one on an anecdote doing the rounds in Ireland: Fr Martin D'Arcy SJ said that the incident happened to his great-grand-aunt and told it to Evelyn Waugh, who turned it into a short story called 'Bella Fleace Gave a Party'. Though Wilde had no 'Aunt Jane' himself, his mother did: Jane Elgee of Wexford, born in 1787. It's perhaps no coincidence that Wilde's mother (also Jane) attracted ridicule in later life for her bizarre attempts to carry on entertaining in the grand style.

Poor Aunt Jane was very old and very proud, and she lived all alone in a splendid, desolate house in County Tipperary. None of her neighbours ever called on Aunt Jane and, had they done so, she would not have been pleased to see them. For she did not want anyone to see the overgrown drives of her estate, or the house with its faded chintzes and suites of shuttered rooms. And she could not bear the idea of anyone discovering that she herself was no longer a toast and a beauty, no longer a power in the countryside, but merely a lonely old woman who had outlived her day.

And so, from year to year she sat alone in her twilight, knowing nothing of the world outside. But one winter, even Aunt Jane became aware of a stir in the air, a wave of excitement that was sweeping over the neighbourhood. New people were coming into the house on the hill, and they were going to give a great Ball, the like of which had never been seen. For the Ryans were enormously rich and — 'The Ryans?' said Aunt Jane. 'I don't know the Ryans. Where do they come from?' Then the terrible blow fell: the Ryans came from nowhere in particular and were reported on good authority to be 'in business'.

'But,' said Aunt Jane, 'what are the poor creatures thinking of? Who will ever go to their ball?' 'Everybody will go,' she was assured. 'Everybody has accepted. It will be a wonderful affair.'

When Aunt Jane heard this, her wrath was terrible. This is what things had come to in the neighbourhood! And, of course, it was all her fault. After all, it had been for her to take the lead, but she had brooded in her tent when she should have been up doing battle.

Then Aunt Jane made a great resolution.

She would give a Ball — a Ball the like of which had never been imagined: she would re-enter Society and show how a grande dame of the old school could really entertain. If the County had so far forgotten itself, she herself would rescue it from those impertinent interlopers.

And so she instantly set to work. The old house was repainted and refurnished, and the grounds were replanted; the supper and the band were ordered from London and an army of waiters was engaged. She was determined that everything should be of the best — and that there should be no question of cost. She told herself that everything would eventually be paid for, even if she had to devote the rest of her life to paying for it.

At last, the great night arrived. The estate was lit for miles around with coloured lamps, the hall and the staircase were gorgeous with flowers, and the dancing floor was as smooth and shiny as a mirror. Then, from their places, the musicians bowed deeply as Aunt Jane, in a splendid gown embroidered with diamonds, descended in state and stood at the ballroom door.

There she waited. And, as time went on, the footmen in the hall and the waiters in the supper-room began to look at each other, and the band tuned up two or three times to show its zeal, but no guests arrived.

And still Aunt Jane, in her beautiful gown, waited at the ballroom door. The clock struck eleven – twelve – half past twelve and still no guests arrived.

At last, Aunt Jane swept a deep curtsy to the band. 'Pray go and have your supper,' she said. 'No one is coming.' Then she went upstairs and died. That is to say, she never again spoke a word to anyone and was dead within three days.

And not for some time after her death was it discovered that Aunt Jane had quite forgotten to send out any invitations.

IMPRESSION DU MATIN

Wilde's friendly rivalry with the American artist and dandy, James Abbott McNeill Whistler, may lie behind this very visual poem (first published in 1881). The painter insisted that a picture should be simply a composition of colour and mood and had no need to tell a story; Wilde, however, was rarely content without movement and anecdote, and here the final stanza suddenly zooms in on a private moment, bringing personality and bite to what might otherwise have remained a verbal pastiche of an Impressionist painting. The title means, simply, 'Impression of the Morning'.

The Thames nocturne of blue and gold
   Changed to a Harmony in grey:
   A barge with ochre-coloured hay
Dropt from the wharf: and chill and cold

The yellow fog came creeping down
   The bridges, till the houses' walls
   Seemed changed to shadows and St. Paul's
Loomed like a bubble o'er the town.

Then suddenly arose the clang
   Of waking life; the streets were stirred
   With country waggons: and a bird
Flew to the glistening roofs and sang.

But one pale woman all alone,
   The daylight kissing her wan hair,
   Loitered beneath the gas lamps' flare,
With lips of flame and heart of stone.

From 'LORD ARTHUR SAVILE'S CRIME'

'Lord Arthur Savile's Crime' began life as one of Wilde's popular after-dinner tales. At a palm-reading conducted by Mr Podgers, the cheiromantist, Lord Arthur is told that he is going to commit a murder one day. Knowing that it would be grossly unfair to wed his beloved Sybil with the terrible prospect of such a crime hanging over the marriage, he resolves to kill someone – anyone – as soon as possible. But, despite his best efforts, his intended victims will not die – indeed, they do not even notice his attempts to do away with them.

When he got upstairs, he flung himself on a sofa, and his eyes filled with tears. He had done his best to commit this murder, but on both occasions he had failed, and through no fault of his own. He had tried to do his duty, but it seemed as if Destiny herself had turned traitor. He was oppressed with the sense of the barrenness of good intentions, of the futility of trying to be fine. Perhaps it would be better to break off the marriage altogether. Sybil would suffer, it is true, but suffering could not really mar a nature so noble as hers. As for himself, what did it matter? There is always some war in which a man can die, some cause to which a man can give his life, and, as life had no pleasure for him, so death had no terror. Let Destiny work out his doom. He would not stir to help her.

At half past seven he dressed, and went down to the club. Surbiton was there with a party of young men, and he was obliged to dine with them. Their trivial conversation and idle jests did not interest him, and as soon as coffee was brought he left them, inventing some engagement in order to get away. As he was going out of the club, the hall-porter handed him a letter. It was from Herr Winckelkopf, asking him to call down the next evening and look at an explosive umbrella that went off as soon as it was opened. It was the very latest invention, and had just arrived from Geneva. He tore the letter up into fragments. He had made up his mind not to try any more experiments. Then he wandered down to the Thames Embankment, and sat for hours by the river. The moon peered through a mane of tawny clouds, as if it were a lion's eye, and innumerable stars spangled the hollow vault, like gold dust powdered on a purple dome. Now and then a barge swung out into the turbid stream and floated away with the tide, and the railway signals changed from green to scarlet as the trains ran shrieking across the bridge. After some time, twelve o'clock boomed from the tall tower at Westminster, and at each stroke of the sonorous bell the night seemed to tremble. Then the railway lights went out, one solitary lamp left gleaming like a large ruby on a giant mast, and the roar of the city became fainter.

At two o'clock he got up, and strolled towards Blackfriars. How unreal everything looked! How like a strange dream! The houses on the other side of the river seemed built out of darkness. One would have said that silver and shadow had fashioned the world anew. The huge dome of St. Paul's loomed like a bubble through the dusky air.

As he approached Cleopatra's Needle he saw a man leaning over the parapet, and as he came nearer the man looked up, the gas-light falling full upon his face.

It was Mr. Podgers, the cheiromantist! No one could mistake the fat, flabby face, the gold-rimmed spectacles, the sickly feeble smile, the sensual mouth.

Lord Arthur stopped. A brilliant idea flashed across him, and he stole softly up behind. In a moment he had seized Mr. Podgers by the legs, and flung him into the Thames. There was a coarse oath, a heavy splash, and all was still. Lord Arthur looked anxiously over, but could see nothing of the cheiromantist but a tall hat, pirouetting in an eddy of moonlit water. After a time it also sank, and no trace of Mr. Podgers was visible. Once he thought that he caught sight of the bulky misshapen figure striking out for the staircase by the bridge, and a horrible feeling of failure came over him, but it turned out to be merely a reflection, and when the moon shone out from behind a cloud it passed away. At last he seemed to have realised the decree of destiny. He heaved a deep sigh of relief, and Sybil's name came to his lips.

'Have you dropped anything, sir?' said a voice behind him suddenly.

He turned round, and saw a policeman with a bull's-eye lantern.

'Nothing of importance, sergeant,' he answered, smiling, and, hailing a passing hansom, he jumped in and told the man to drive to Belgrave Square.

For the next few days he alternated between hope and fear. There were moments when he almost expected Mr. Podgers to walk into the room, and yet at other times he felt that Fate could not be so unjust to him. Twice he went to the cheiromantist's address in West Moon Street, but he could not bring himself to ring the bell. He longed for certainty, and was afraid of it.

Finally it came. He was sitting in the smoking-room of the club having tea, and listening rather wearily to Surbiton's account of the last comic song at the Gaiety, when the waiter came in with the evening papers. He took up the *St. James's*, and was listlessly turning over its pages, when this strange heading caught his eye:

'SUICIDE OF A CHEIROMANTIST'

He turned pale with excitement, and began to read. The paragraph ran as follows:

'Yesterday morning, at seven o'clock, the body of Mr. Septimus R. Podgers, the eminent cheiromantist, was washed on shore at Greenwich, just in front of the Ship Hotel. The unfortunate gentleman had been missing for some days, and considerable anxiety for his safety had been felt in cheiromantic circles. It is supposed that he committed suicide under the influence of a temporary mental derangement, caused by overwork, and a verdict to that effect was returned this afternoon by the coroner's jury. Mr. Podgers had just completed an elaborate treatise on the subject of the Human Hand, that will shortly be published, when it will no doubt attract much attention. The deceased was sixty-five years of age, and does not seem to have left any relations.'

Lord Arthur rushed out of the club with the paper still in his hand, to the immense amazement of the hall-porter, who tried in vain to stop him, and drove at once to Park Lane. Sybil saw him from the window, and something told her that he was the bearer of good news. She ran down to meet him, and, when she saw his face, she knew that all was well.

'My dear Sybil,' cried Lord Arthur, 'let us be married to-morrow!'

'You foolish boy! Why, the cake is not even ordered!' said Sybil, laughing through her tears.

DISOBEDIENCE IS MAN'S ORIGINAL VIRTUE
PIONEER OF DECADENCE, AGENT PROVOCATEUR

THE DOER OF GOOD

To an enquiry about his religion, Wilde replied, 'Well, you know, I don't think I have any. I am an Irish Protestant.' While at Oxford he flirted with the 'bells and smells' of Roman Catholicism, and later became fascinated with the humanity and personality of Jesus Christ. 'His entire life is the most wonderful of poems,' he said. 'He is just like a work of art Himself.' Several of his 'Poems in Prose' read like biblical parables, exploring the individualism of Jesus and the paradoxes of His life.

I t was night-time and He was alone.

And He saw afar-off the walls of a round city and went towards the city.

And when He came near He heard within the city the tread of the feet of joy, and the laughter of the mouth of gladness and the loud noise of many lutes. And He knocked at the gate and certain of the gate-keepers opened to Him.

And He beheld a house that was of marble and had fair pillars of marble before it. The pillars were hung with garlands, and within and without there were torches of cedar. And He entered the house.

And when He had passed through the hall of chalcedony and the hall of jasper, and reached the long hall of feasting, He saw lying on a couch of sea-purple one whose hair was crowned with red roses and whose lips were red with wine.

And He went behind him and touched him on the shoulder and said to him, 'Why do you live like this?'

And the young man turned round and recognised Him, and made answer and said, 'But I was a leper once, and you healed me. How else should I live?'

And He passed out of the house and went again into the street.

And after a little while He saw one whose face and raiment were painted and whose feet were shod with pearls. And behind her came, slowly as a hunter, a young man who wore a cloak of two colours. Now the face of the woman was as the fair face of an idol, and the eyes of the young man were bright with lust.

And He followed swiftly and touched the hand of the young man and said to him, 'Why do you look at this woman and in such wise?'

And the young man turned round and recognised Him and said, 'But I was blind once, and you gave me sight. At what else should I look?'

And He ran forward and touched the painted raiment of the woman and said to her, 'Is there no other way to walk save the way of sin?'

And the woman turned round and recognised Him, and laughed and said, 'But you forgave me my sins, and the way is a pleasant way.'

And He passed out of the city.

And when He had passed out of the city He saw seated by the roadside a young man who was weeping.

And He went towards him and touched the long locks of his hair and said to him, 'Why are you weeping?'

And the young man looked up and recognised Him and made answer, 'But I was dead once, and you raised me from the dead. What else should I do but weep?'

THE HARLOT'S HOUSE

'The Harlot's House' is one of the most hauntingly evocative of Wilde's poems. It was written in Paris in 1883 during a break between lecture tours. A *danse macabre*, or 'dance of death', is in progress to the strains of a waltz by Johann Strauss, ironically entitled the 'Treues Liebes Herz' ('The Heart of True Love'). Curiously, a tune of that title has proved impossible to find, and it may well be Wilde's invention. The verses caused, as one biographer has commented, 'some stir at the time because it was not the custom for Victorian poets to write on brothels'.

We caught the tread of dancing feet,
We loitered down the moonlit street,
And stopped beneath the harlot's house.

Inside, above the din and fray,
We heard the loud musicians play
The 'Treues Liebes Herz' of Strauss.

Like strange mechanical grotesques,
Making fantastic arabesques,
The shadows raced across the blind.

We watched the ghostly dancers spin
To sound of horn and violin,
Like black leaves wheeling in the wind.

Like wire-pulled automatons,
Slim silhouetted skeletons
Went sidling through the slow quadrille,

They took each other by the hand,
And danced a stately saraband;
Their laughter echoed thin and shrill.

Sometimes a clockwork puppet pressed
A phantom lover to her breast,
Sometimes they seemed to try to sing.

Sometimes a horrible marionette
Came out, and smoked its cigarette
Upon the steps like a live thing.

Then, turning to my love, I said,
'The dead are dancing with the dead,
The dust is whirling with the dust.'

But she – she heard the violin,
And left my side, and entered in:
Love passed into the house of lust.

Then suddenly the tune went false,
The dancers wearied of the waltz,
The shadows ceased to wheel and whirl.

And down the long and silent street,
The dawn, with silver-sandalled feet,
Crept like a frightened girl.

From SALOMÉ

The one-act play *Salomé* was written in French. It is based on the
biblical tale about the death of John the Baptist (called Jokanaan
in Wilde's version). It was never staged in England during the
author's lifetime, for, as Wilde put it to a correspondent, 'the
refusal of the Licenser to allow the performance of my tragedy
was based entirely on his silly vulgar rule about no biblical subject
being treated'. However, in 1893, an English translation appeared
in book form with astonishing illustrations by Aubrey Beardsley –
though one had to be omitted, for reasons described by the artist
in a verse: 'Because one figure was undressed / This little drawing
was suppressed. / It was unkind. But never mind, / Perhaps it was
all for the best.' *Salomé* was staged in Paris in 1896, but the ban
meant that it did not have its first public performance in England
until 1931.

SALOMÉ: JOKANAAN!

JOKANAAN: Who is speaking?

SALOMÉ: Jokanaan, I lust for your body! Your body is white like the lilies of a field that the mower has never mowed. Your body is white like the snows that lie on the mountains, like the snows that lie on the mountains of Judaea, and come down into the valleys. The roses in the garden of the Queen of Arabia are not as white as your body. Neither the roses in the garden of the Queen of Arabia, nor the feet of the dawn when they alight on the leaves, nor the breast of the moon as it lies on the breast of the sea. ... There is nothing in the world as white as your body. Let me touch your body.

JOKANAAN: Back, daughter of Babylon! Evil was brought into the world by Woman. Do not speak to me. I will not listen to you. I listen only to the voice of the Lord God.

SALOMÉ: Your body is hideous. It is like the body of a leper. It is like a plastered wall where vipers have crawled; like a plastered wall where the scorpions have made their nest. It is like a whitened sepulchre full of disgusting things. It is horrible, your body is horrible. ... Your hair is what attracts me, Jokanaan. Your hair is like clusters of grapes, like the clusters of black grapes that hang from the vines of Edom in the land of the Edomites. Your hair is like the cedars of Lebanon, like the great cedars of Lebanon that give their shade to the lions and to the robbers who wish to hide themselves by day. The long black nights, the nights when the moon hides her face, when the stars are afraid, are not as black. The silence that dwells in the forest is not as black. There is nothing in the world as black as your hair. ... Let me touch your hair.

JOKANAAN: Back, daughter of Sodom! Do not touch me. Do not profane the temple of the Lord God.

SALOMÉ: Your hair is horrible. It is covered with mud and dust. It is like a crown of thorns which they have placed on your forehead. It is like a knot of black snakes writhing round your neck. I do not love your hair. ... It is your mouth that I desire, Jokanaan. Your mouth is like a thread of scarlet on a tower of ivory. It is like a pomegranate cut with a knife of ivory. The pomegranate-flowers that blossom in the gardens of Tyre, and are redder than roses, are not as red. The red blasts of trumpets that herald the approach of kings, and terrify the enemy, are not as red. Your mouth is redder than the feet of those who tread the wine in the wine-press. Your mouth is redder than the feet of the doves that haunt the temples and are fed by the priests. It is redder than the feet of a man who comes from a forest where he has slain a lion and seen gilded tigers. Your mouth is like a branch of coral that the fishers have found in the twilight of the sea, the coral that they keep for kings! ... It is like the vermilion that the Moabites find in the mines of Moab, the vermilion that the kings take from them. It is like the bow of the King of the Persians, which is painted with vermilion and tipped with coral. There is nothing in the world as red as your mouth. ... Let me kiss your mouth.

JOKANAAN: Never, daughter of Babylon! Daughter of Sodom, never!

SALOMÉ: I will kiss your mouth, Jokanaan. I will kiss your mouth.

IN FULL PURSUIT

PLAYWRIGHT, SOCIAL COMMENTATOR AND WIT

A FEW MAXIMS FOR THE INSTRUCTION OF THE OVER-EDUCATED

In 1894, Frank Harris, editor of the *Saturday Review*, published these nuggets of wisdom and wit. They appeared anonymously and have only relatively recently been recognised as Wilde's work. Like the Preface to *The Picture of Dorian Gray*, which opens this book, most of these aphorisms are much more than witty phrases or knowing jokes – they are acute observations of the contradictions of modern life, effortlessly identifying truths that might have furnished a lesser writer with a lifetime of themes.

Education is an admirable thing. But it is well to remember from time to time that nothing that is worth knowing can be taught.

Public opinion exists only where there are no ideas.

The English are always degrading truths into facts. When a truth becomes a fact it loses all its intellectual value.

It is a very sad thing that nowadays there is so little useless information.

The only link between Literature and Drama left to us in England at the present moment is the bill of the play.

In old days books were written by men of letters and read by the public. Nowadays books are written by the public and read by nobody.

Most women are so artificial that they have no sense of Art. Most men are so natural that they have no sense of Beauty.

Friendship is far more tragic than love. It lasts longer.

What is abnormal in Life stands in normal relations to Art. It is the only thing in Life that stands in normal relations to Art.

A subject that is beautiful in itself gives no suggestion to the artist. It lacks imperfection.

The only thing that the artist cannot see is the obvious. The only thing that the public can see is the obvious. The result is the Criticism of the Journalist.

Art is the only serious thing in the world. And the artist is the only person who is never serious.

To be really mediæval one should have no body. To be really modern one should have no soul. To be really Greek one should have no clothes.

Dandyism is the assertion of the absolute modernity of Beauty.

The only thing that can console one for being poor is extravagance. The only thing that can console one for being rich is economy.

One should never listen. To listen is a sign of indifference to one's hearers.

Even the disciple has his uses. He stands behind one's throne, and at the moment of one's triumph whispers in one's ear that, after all, one is immortal.

The criminal classes are so close to us that even the policemen can see them. They are so far away from us that only the poet can understand them.

Those whom the gods love grow young.

From *LADY WINDERMERE'S FAN*

'The only link between Literature and Drama left to us in England at the present moment is the bill of the play.' Wilde wasn't entirely joking: if playbills (theatre programmes) were closer to high art than anything on stage, the theatre in the 1890s was in a sorry state. However, he had been doing something about it himself, by writing the first of his 'social comedies'. When *Lady Windermere's Fan* had a runaway success, it was obvious that Wilde had found a way to display his skills to the full.

Wilde's first-night speech from the stage is still quoted: 'Ladies and gentlemen: I have enjoyed this evening immensely. The actors have given us a charming rendering of a delightful play, and your appreciation has been most intelligent. I congratulate you on the great success of your performance, which persuades me that you think almost as highly of the play as I do myself.'

DUCHESS OF BERWICK: Agatha, darling!

LADY AGATHA (*entering*): Yes, mamma.

DUCHESS OF BERWICK: Come and bid good-bye to Lady Windermere, and thank her for your charming visit. (*To* LADY WINDERMERE.) And by the way, I must thank you for sending a card to Mr. Hopper – he's that rich young Australian people are taking such notice of just at present. His father made a great fortune by selling some kind of food in circular tins – most palatable, I believe – I fancy it is the thing the servants always refuse to eat. But the son is quite interesting. I think he's attracted by dear Agatha's clever talk. Of course, we should be very sorry to lose her, but I think that a mother who doesn't part with a daughter every season has no real affection. We're coming to-night, dear. And remember my advice, take the poor fellow out of town at once, it is the only thing to do. Good-bye, once more; come, Agatha. (*Exeunt* DUCHESS *and* LADY AGATHA.) [...]

HOPPER: How do you do, Lady Windermere? How do you do, Duchess? (Bows to LADY AGATHA.)

DUCHESS OF BERWICK: Dear Mr. Hopper, how nice of you to come so early. We all know how you are run after in London.

HOPPER: Capital place, London! They are not nearly so exclusive in London as they are in Sydney.

DUCHESS OF BERWICK: Ah! we know your value, Mr. Hopper. We wish there were more like you. It would make life so much easier. Do you know, Mr. Hopper, dear Agatha and I are so much interested in Australia. It must be so pretty with all the dear little kangaroos flying about. Agatha has found it on the map. What a curious shape it is! Just like a large packing case. However, it is a very young country, isn't it?

HOPPER: Wasn't it made at the same time as the others, Duchess?

DUCHESS OF BERWICK: How clever you are, Mr. Hopper. You have a cleverness quite of your own. Now I mustn't keep you.

HOPPER: But I should like to dance with Lady Agatha, Duchess.

DUCHESS OF BERWICK: Well, I *hope* she has a dance left. Have you a dance left, Agatha?

LADY AGATHA: Yes, mamma.

DUCHESS OF BERWICK: The next one?

LADY AGATHA: Yes, mamma.

HOPPER: May I have the pleasure? (LADY AGATHA *bows.*)

DUCHESS OF BERWICK: Mind you take great care of my little chatter-box, Mr. Hopper.

LADY AGATHA *and* MR. HOPPER *pass into ballroom.* […]

DUCHESS OF BERWICK: But where is Agatha? Oh, there she is. (LADY AGATHA *and* MR. HOPPER *enter from terrace.*) Mr. Hopper, I am very, very angry with you. You have taken Agatha out on the terrace, and she is so delicate.

HOPPER: Awfully sorry, Duchess. We went out for a moment and then got chatting together.

DUCHESS OF BERWICK: Ah, about dear Australia, I suppose?

HOPPER: Yes!

DUCHESS OF BERWICK: Agatha, darling! (*Beckons her over.*)

LADY AGATHA: Yes, mamma!

DUCHESS OF BERWICK (*aside*): Did Mr. Hopper definitely—

LADY AGATHA: Yes, mamma.

74

DUCHESS OF BERWICK: And what answer did you give him, dear child?

LADY AGATHA: Yes, mamma.

DUCHESS OF BERWICK (*affectionately*): My dear one! You always say the right thing. Mr. Hopper! James! Agatha has told me everything. How cleverly you have both kept your secret.

HOPPER: You don't mind my taking Agatha off to Australia, then, Duchess?

DUCHESS OF BERWICK (*indignantly*): To Australia? Oh, don't mention that dreadful vulgar place.

HOPPER: But she said she'd like to come with me.

DUCHESS OF BERWICK (*severely*): Did you say that, Agatha?

LADY AGATHA: Yes, mamma.

DUCHESS OF BERWICK: Agatha, you say the most silly things possible. I think on the whole that Grosvenor Square would be a more healthy place to reside in. There are lots of vulgar people live in Grosvenor Square, but at any rate there are no horrid kangaroos crawling about. But we'll talk about that to-morrow. James, you can take Agatha down. You'll come to lunch, of course, James. At half past one, instead of two. The Duke will wish to say a few words to you, I am sure.

HOPPER: I should like to have a chat with the Duke, Duchess. He has not said a single word to me yet.

DUCHESS OF BERWICK: I think you'll find he will have a great deal to say to you to-morrow. (*Exit* LADY AGATHA *with* MR. HOPPER. *To* LADY WINDERMERE.) And now good-night, Margaret. I'm afraid it's the old, old story, dear. Love – well, not love at first sight, but love at the end of the season, which is so much more satisfactory.

From THE SOUL OF MAN UNDER SOCIALISM

The modernity of Wilde's political thought is striking. In his long essay, *The Soul of Man under Socialism*, he sums up what many still feel is wrong with capitalism. With characteristic irony he dismisses the attempts of well-meaning activists and philanthropists to close the gap between rich and poor, for such imbalances are essential to the system of market economics. Wilde was writing before socialism (or communism) had been seriously attempted, but within a few decades his remarks on the dangers of state tyranny would be hideously illustrated in Stalinist Russia. His challenge, to devise a system of living that balances freedom with individualism and Christian ideals with pleasure, is one that remains today.

The chief advantage that would result from the establishment of Socialism is, undoubtedly, the fact that Socialism would relieve us from that sordid necessity of living for others which, in the present condition of things, presses so hardly upon almost everybody. In fact, scarcely anyone at all escapes. [...]

The majority of people spoil their lives by an unhealthy and exaggerated altruism — are forced, indeed, so to spoil them. They find themselves surrounded by hideous poverty, by hideous ugliness, by hideous starvation. It is inevitable that they should be strongly moved by all this. [...] Accordingly, with admirable, though misdirected intentions, they very seriously and very sentimentally set themselves to the task of remedying the evils that they see. But their remedies do not cure the disease: they merely prolong it. Indeed, their remedies are part of the disease.

They try to solve the problem of poverty, for instance, by keeping the poor alive; or, in the case of a very advanced school, by amusing the poor.

But this is not a solution: it is an aggravation of the difficulty. The proper aim is to try and reconstruct society on such a basis that poverty will be impossible. And the altruistic virtues have really prevented the carrying out of this aim. Just as the worst slave-owners were those who were kind to their slaves, and so prevented the horror of the system being realised by those who suffered from it, and understood by those who contemplated it, so, in the present state of things in England, the people who do most harm are the people who try to do most good; and at last we have had the spectacle of men who have really studied the problem and know the life — educated men who live in the East End — coming forward and imploring the community to restrain its altruistic impulses of charity, benevolence, and the like. They do so on the ground that such charity degrades and demoralises. They are perfectly right. Charity creates a multitude of sins.

There is also this to be said. It is immoral to use private property in order to alleviate the horrible evils that result from the institution of private property. It is both immoral and unfair.

Under Socialism all this will, of course, be altered. There will be no people living in fetid dens and fetid rags, and bringing up unhealthy, hunger-pinched children in the midst of impossible and absolutely repulsive surroundings. The security of society will not depend, as it does now, on the state of the weather. If a frost comes we shall not have a hundred thousand men out of work, tramping about the streets in a state of disgusting misery, or whining to their neighbours for alms, or crowding round the doors of loathsome shelters to try and secure a hunch of bread and a night's unclean lodging. Each member of the society will share in the general prosperity and happiness of the society, and if a frost comes no one will practically be anything the worse. [...]

Socialism, Communism, or whatever one chooses to call it, by converting private property into public wealth, and substituting co-operation for competition, will restore society to its proper condition of a thoroughly healthy organism, and insure the material well-being of each member of the community. It will, in fact, give Life its proper basis and its proper environment. But for the full development of Life to its highest mode of perfection, something more is needed. What is needed is Individualism. If the Socialism is Authoritarian; if there are Governments armed with economic power as they are now with political power; if, in a word, we are to have Industrial Tyrannies, then the last state of man will be worse than the first. [...]

We are often told that the poor are grateful for charity. Some of them are, no doubt, but the best amongst the poor are never grateful. They are ungrateful, discontented, disobedient, and rebellious. They are quite right to be so. Charity they feel to be a ridiculously inadequate mode of partial restitution, or a sentimental dole, usually accompanied by some impertinent attempt on the part of the sentimentalist to tyrannise over their private lives. Why should they be grateful for the crumbs that fall from the rich man's table? They should be seated at the board, and are beginning to know it. As for being discontented, a man who would not be discontented with such surroundings and such a low mode of life would be a perfect brute. Disobedience, in the eyes of anyone who has read history, is man's original virtue. It is through disobedience that progress has been made, through disobedience and through rebellion. [...]

As for the virtuous poor, one can pity them, of course, but one cannot possibly admire them. They have made private terms with the enemy, and sold their birthright for very bad pottage. They must also be extraordinarily stupid. I can quite understand a man accepting laws that protect private property, and admit of its accumulation, as long as he himself is able under those conditions to realise some form of beautiful and intellectual life. But it is almost incredible to me how a man whose life is marred and made hideous by such laws can possibly acquiesce in their continuance.

However, the explanation is not really difficult to find. It is simply this. Misery and poverty are so absolutely degrading, and exercise such a paralysing effect over the nature of men, that no class is ever really conscious of its own suffering. They have to be told of it by other people, and they often entirely disbelieve them. [...]

It is clear, then, that no Authoritarian Socialism will do. For while under the present system a very large number of people can lead lives of a certain amount of freedom and expression and happiness, under an industrial-barrack system, or a system of economic tyranny, nobody would be able to have any such freedom at all. It is to be regretted that a portion of our community should be practically in slavery, but to propose to solve the problem by enslaving the entire community is childish. Every man must be left quite free to choose his own work. No form of compulsion must be exercised over him. If there is, his work will not be good for him, will not be good in itself, and will not be good for others. And by work I simply mean activity of any kind. […]

But it may be asked how Individualism, which is now more or less dependent on the existence of private property for its development, will benefit by the abolition of such private property. […] It will benefit in this way. Under the new conditions Individualism will be far freer, far finer, and far more intensified than it is now. […] For the recognition of private property has really harmed Individualism, and obscured it, by confusing a man with what he possesses. It has led Individualism entirely astray. It has made gain not growth its aim. So that man thought that the important thing was to have, and did not know that the important thing is to be. The true perfection of man lies, not in what man has, but in what man is.

From A WOMAN OF NO IMPORTANCE

At first glance, *A Woman of No Importance* seems to be just another Victorian melodrama with added humour, but behind the sparkle and laughter lie the seeds of social revolution. The play is driven by satirical portrayals of the usually unquestioned norms and attitudes of society: the subservient place of women, the assumed immorality of sexual nonconformity, the acceptance of the status conferred by class and wealth. Wilde's revolutionary subtexts, delivered via a wit that his countryman George Bernard Shaw saw as characteristically Irish, reveal him to be an important radical – even anarchist – thinker.

LORD ILLINGWORTH: I took a great fancy to young Arbuthnot the moment I met him, and he'll be of considerable use to me in something I am foolish enough to think of doing.

LADY HUNSTANTON: He is an admirable young man. And his mother is one of my dearest friends. He has just gone for a walk with our pretty American. She is very pretty, is she not?

LADY CAROLINE: Far too pretty. These American girls carry off all the good matches. Why can't they stay in their own country? They are always telling us it is the Paradise of women.

LORD ILLINGWORTH: It is, Lady Caroline. That is why, like Eve, they are so extremely anxious to get out of it.

LADY CAROLINE: Who are Miss Worsley's parents?

LORD ILLINGWORTH: American women are wonderfully clever in concealing their parents.

LADY HUNSTANTON: My dear Lord Illingworth, what do you mean? Miss Worsley, Caroline, is an orphan. Her father was a very wealthy millionaire or philanthropist, or both, I believe, who entertained my son quite hospitably, when he visited Boston. I don't know how he made his money, originally.

KELVIL: I fancy in American dry goods.

LADY HUNSTANTON: What are American dry goods?

LORD ILLINGWORTH: American novels.

LADY HUNSTANTON: How very singular! ... Well, from whatever source her large fortune came, I have a great esteem for Miss Worsley. She dresses exceedingly well. All Americans do dress well. They get their clothes in Paris.

MRS. ALLONBY: They say, Lady Hunstanton, that when good Americans die they go to Paris.

LADY HUNSTANTON: Indeed? And when bad Americans die, where do they go to?

LORD ILLINGWORTH: Oh, they go to America.

KELVIL: I am afraid you don't appreciate America, Lord Illingworth. It is a very remarkable country, especially considering its youth.

LORD ILLINGWORTH: The youth of America is their oldest tradition. It has been going on now for three hundred years. To hear them talk one would imagine they were in their first childhood. As far as civilisation goes they are in their second.

KELVIL: There is undoubtedly a great deal of corruption in American politics. I suppose you allude to that?

LORD ILLINGWORTH: I wonder.

LADY HUNSTANTON: Politics are in a sad way everywhere, I am told. They certainly are in England. Dear Mr. Cardew is ruining the country. I wonder Mrs. Cardew allows him. I am sure, Lord Illingworth, you don't think that uneducated people should be allowed to have votes?

LORD ILLINGWORTH: I think they are the only people who should.

KELVIL: Do you take no side then in modern politics, Lord Illingworth?

LORD ILLINGWORTH: One should never take sides in anything, Mr. Kelvil. Taking sides is the beginning of sincerity, and earnestness follows shortly afterwards, and the human being becomes a bore. However, the House of Commons really does very little harm. You can't make people good by Act of Parliament — that is something.

KELVIL: You cannot deny that the House of Commons has always shown great sympathy with the sufferings of the poor.

LORD ILLINGWORTH: That is its special vice. That is the special vice of the age. One should sympathise with the joy, the beauty, the colour of life. The less said about life's sores the better, Mr. Kelvil.

KELVIL: Still, our East End is a very important problem.

LORD ILLINGWORTH: Quite so. It is the problem of slavery. And we are trying to solve it by amusing the slaves.

LADY HUNSTANTON: Certainly, a great deal may be done by means of cheap entertainments, as you say, Lord Illingworth. Dear Dr. Daubeny, our rector here, provides, with the assistance of his curates, really admirable recreations for the poor during the winter. And much good may be done by means of a magic lantern, or a missionary, or some popular amusement of that kind.

LADY CAROLINE: I am not at all in favour of amusements for the poor, Jane. Blankets and coals are sufficient. There is too much love of pleasure amongst the upper classes as it is. Health is what we want in modern life. The tone is not healthy, not healthy at all.

MRS. ALLONBY: Horrid word, 'health'.

LORD ILLINGWORTH: Silliest word in our language, and one knows so well the popular idea of health. The English country gentleman galloping after a fox—the unspeakable in full pursuit of the uneatable.

From THE IMPORTANCE OF BEING EARNEST

On St Valentine's Day, 1895, what was to become Wilde's most famous play opened in London to a keenly enthusiastic reception. Such was the play's sparkle and spirit that reviewers, though they enjoyed it as much as anyone, were left groping for anything profound to say about it. The eminent theatrical columnist and essayist William Archer, for example, commented, 'it sends wave after wave of laughter curling and foaming around the theatre, but as a text for criticism it is barren and delusive ... What can a poor critic do?'

On the evening of that triumphant first performance, there was an embarrassing incident in the foyer of the theatre. The Marquess of Queensberry, the outraged father of 'Bosie', Lord Alfred Douglas, with whom Wilde was now unashamedly in love, appeared, intending to disrupt the play. Police were on hand, so Queensbury had to content himself with leaving a 'grotesque bouquet of vegetables' for the playwright. The incident marked the beginning of the end for Wilde's career and reputation. Two months later, the antagonists were facing each other in court in the first of three trials, which culminated in Wilde's imprisonment for homosexual offences. *The Importance of Being Earnest* continued its run, but with the author's name removed from the billing.

Almost three generations were to pass before academic commentators began to appreciate the complexity and subtlety of Wilde's masterpiece. In the meantime, the popularity of the play scarcely slackened; since that memorable first night it has been in almost continuous performance, entertaining many millions of people in theatres (and cinemas) around the world. The extract below is taken from what is probably the author's most celebrated scene.

LADY BRACKNELL (*sitting down*): You can take a seat, Mr. Worthing. (*Looks in her pocket for note-book and pencil.*)

JACK: Thank you, Lady Bracknell, I prefer standing.

LADY BRACKNELL (*pencil and note-book in hand*): I feel bound to tell you that you are not down on my list of eligible young men, although I have the same list as the dear Duchess of Bolton has. We work together, in fact. However, I am quite ready to enter your name, should your answers be what a really affectionate mother requires. Do you smoke?

JACK: Well, yes, I must admit I smoke.

LADY BRACKNELL: I am glad to hear it. A man should always have an occupation of some kind. There are far too many idle men in London as it is. How old are you?

JACK: Twenty-nine.

LADY BRACKNELL: A very good age to be married at. I have always been of opinion that a man who desires to get married should know either everything or nothing. Which do you know?

JACK (*after some hesitation*): I know nothing, Lady Bracknell.

LADY BRACKNELL: I am pleased to hear it. I do not approve of anything that tampers with natural ignorance. Ignorance is like a delicate exotic fruit; touch it and the bloom is gone. The whole theory of modern education is radically unsound. Fortunately in England, at any rate, education produces no effect whatsoever. If it did, it would prove a serious danger to the upper classes, and probably lead to acts of violence in Grosvenor Square. What is your income?

JACK: Between seven and eight thousand a year.

LADY BRACKNELL (*makes a note in her book*): In land, or in investments?

JACK: In investments, chiefly.

LADY BRACKNELL: That is satisfactory. What between the duties expected of one during one's lifetime, and the duties exacted from one after one's death, land has ceased to be either a profit or a pleasure. It gives one position, and prevents one from keeping it up. That's all that can be said about land.

JACK: I have a country house with some land, of course, attached to it, about fifteen hundred acres, I believe; but

I don't depend on that for my real income. In fact, as far as I can make out, the poachers are the only people who make anything out of it.

LADY BRACKNELL: A country house! How many bedrooms (JACK, *in a puzzled kind of way, begins to count on his fingers.*) Well, that point can be cleared up afterwards. You have a town house, I hope? A girl with a simple, unspoiled nature, like Gwendolen, could hardly be expected to reside in the country.

JACK: Well, I own a house in Belgrave Square, but it is let by the year to Lady Bloxham. Of course, I can get it back whenever I like, at six months' notice.

LADY BRACKNELL: Lady Bloxham? I don't know her.

JACK: Oh, she goes about very little. She is a lady considerably advanced in years.

LADY BRACKNELL: Ah, nowadays that is no guarantee of respectability of character. What number in Belgrave Square?

JACK: 149.

LADY BRACKNELL (*shaking her head*): The unfashionable side. I thought there was something. However, that could easily be altered.

JACK: Do you mean the fashion, or the side, Lady Bracknell?

92

LADY BRACKNELL (*sternly*): Both, if necessary, I presume. What are your politics?

JACK: Well, I am afraid I really have none, Lady Bracknell. I am a Liberal Unionist, I believe!

LADY BRACKNELL: Oh, they count as Tories. They dine with us. Or come in the evening, at any rate. Now to minor matters. Are your parents living?

JACK: I have lost both my parents.

LADY BRACKNELL: To lose one parent, Mr Worthing, may be regarded as a misfortune; to lose both looks like carelessness. Who was your father? He was evidently a man of some wealth. Was he born in what the Radical papers call the purple of commerce, or did he rise from the ranks of aristocracy?

JACK: I am afraid I really don't know. The fact is, Lady Bracknell, I said I had lost my parents. It would be nearer the truth to say that my parents seem to have lost me. ... I don't actually know who I am by birth. I was ... well, I was found.

LADY BRACKNELL: Found?

JACK: The late Mr. Thomas Cardew, an old gentleman of a very charitable and kindly disposition, found me, and gave me the name of Worthing, because he happened to have a first-class ticket for Worthing in his pocket at the time. Worthing is a place in Sussex. It is a seaside resort.

LADY BRACKNELL: Where did the charitable gentleman who had a first-class ticket for this seaside resort find you?

JACK (*gravely*): In a hand-bag.

LADY BRACKNELL: A hand-bag?

JACK (*very seriously*): Yes, Lady Bracknell. I was in a hand-bag – a somewhat large, black leather hand-bag, with handles to it – an ordinary hand-bag, in fact.

LADY BRACKNELL: In what locality did this Mr. James, or Thomas, Cardew come across this ordinary hand-bag?

JACK: In the cloak-room at Victoria Station. It was given to him in mistake for his own.

LADY BRACKNELL: The cloak-room at Victoria Station?

JACK: Yes. The Brighton Line.

LADY BRACKNELL: The line is immaterial. Mr. Worthing, I confess I feel somewhat bewildered by what you have just told me. To be born, or at any rate bred, in a hand-bag, whether it had handles or not, seems to me to display a contempt for the ordinary decencies of family life that remind one of the worst excesses of the French Revolution. And I presume you know what that unfortunate movement led to? As for the particular locality in which the hand-bag was found, a cloak-room at a railway station might serve to conceal a social indiscretion – has probably, indeed, been used for that purpose before now – but it could hardly be regarded as an assured basis for a recognised position in good society.

JACK: May I ask you then what you would advise me to do? I need hardly say I would do anything in the world to ensure Gwendolen's happiness.

LADY BRACKNELL: I would strongly advise you, Mr. Worthing, to try and acquire some relations as soon as possible, and to make a definite effort to produce at any rate one parent, of either sex, before the season is quite over.

JACK: Well, I don't see how I could possibly manage to do that. I can produce the hand-bag at any moment. It is in my dressing-room at home. I really think that should satisfy you, Lady Bracknell.

LADY BRACKNELL: Me, sir! What has it to do with me? You can hardly imagine that I and Lord Bracknell would dream of allowing our only daughter – a girl brought up with the utmost care – to marry into a cloak-room, and form an alliance with a parcel. Good-morning, Mr. Worthing!
(LADY BRACKNELL *sweeps out in majestic indignation.*)

THE LOVE THAT DARE NOT SPEAK ITS NAME

SCANDAL AND IMPRISONMENT

WILDE ON TRIAL

Wilde underwent two trials in April 1895, the first when he ill-advisedly took an action for libel against the Marquess of Queensberry, who had suggested that he was an active homosexual. Queensberry's defence was led by Edward Carson, another Irishman. Carson quoted from the Preface to *The Picture of Dorian Gray* ('There is no such thing as a moral or an immoral book. Books are well written, or badly written') but failed to establish that the writer's works proved the foulness of the man. However, when witnesses were found who testified to Wilde's activities, the case was lost.

Homosexual activity being illegal, the second trial became inevitable. Wilde was charged on twenty-five counts of gross indecency and conspiracy. In the course of questioning, he argued that love between two men was a normal and valuable part of human life: under the circumstances, it was perhaps the most courageous and revolutionary statement of his life.

The jury in this second trial failed to reach a verdict, but at the retrial, a month later, the maximum penalty for gross indecency was imposed: two years' hard labour. The judge told the court that the sentence was 'totally inadequate'. According to one report, he ignored the prisoner's response, 'And I? May I say nothing, my lord?' And then the warders took Wilde away.

The following exchange is taken from shorthand reports of the second trial, held on 30 April 1895. The judge, Sir Edward Clarke, has called Wilde to give evidence:

The prisoner rose with seeming alacrity from his place in the dock, walked with a firm tread and dignified demeanour to the witness-box, and leaning across the rail in the same easy and not ungraceful attitude that he assumed when examined by Mr. Carson in the libel action, prepared to answer the questions addressed to him by his counsel. Wilde was first interrogated as to his previous career. In the year 1884, he had married a Miss Lloyd, and from that time to the present he had continued to live with his wife at 16, Tite Street, Chelsea. He also occupied rooms in St. James's Place, which were rented for the purposes of his literary labours, as it was quite impossible to secure quiet and mental repose at his own house, when his two young sons were at home. He had heard the evidence in this case against himself, and asserted that there was no shadow of a foundation for the charges of indecent behaviour alleged against himself. Mr. Gill then rose to cross-examine, and the Court at once became on the *qui vive*. Wilde seemed perfectly calm and did not change his attitude, or tone of polite deprecation.

MR. GILL: You are acquainted with a publication entitled 'The Chameleon'?

WITNESS: Very well indeed.

MR. GILL: Contributors to that journal are friends of yours?

WITNESS: That is so.

MR. GILL: I believe that Lord Alfred Douglas was a frequent contributor?

WITNESS: Hardly that, I think. He wrote some verses occasionally for the 'Chameleon', and, indeed, for other papers.

MR. GILL: The poems in question were somewhat peculiar?

WITNESS: They certainly were not mere commonplaces like so much that is labelled poetry.

MR. GILL: The tone of them met with your critical approval?

WITNESS: It was not for me to approve or disapprove. I leave that to the Reviews.

MR. GILL: At the trial *Queensberry* and *Wilde* you described them as 'beautiful poems'?

WITNESS: I said something tantamount to that. The verses were original in theme and construction, and I admired them.

MR. GILL: In one of the sonnets by Lord A. Douglas, a peculiar use is made of the word 'shame'?

WITNESS: I have noticed the line you refer to.

MR. GILL: What significance would you attach to the use of that word in connection with the idea of the poem?

WITNESS: I can hardly take it upon myself to explain the thoughts of another man.

MR. GILL: You were remarkably friendly with the author? Perhaps he vouchsafed you an explanation?

WITNESS: On one occasion he did.

MR. GILL: I should like to hear it.

WITNESS: Lord Alfred explained that the word 'shame' was used in the sense of modesty, i.e. to feel shame or not to feel shame.

MR. GILL: You can, perhaps, understand that such verses as these would not be acceptable to the reader with an ordinarily balanced mind?

WITNESS: I am not prepared to say. It appears to me to be a question of taste, temperament and individuality. I should say that one man's poetry is another man's poison! [*Loud laughter.*]

MR. GILL: I daresay! There is another sonnet. What construction can be put on the line, 'I am the love that dare not speak its name'?

WITNESS: I think the writer's meaning is quite unambiguous. The love he alluded to was that between an elder and younger man, as between David and Jonathan; such love as Plato made the basis of his philosophy; such as was sung in the sonnets of Shakespeare and Michael Angelo; that deep spiritual affection that was as pure as it was perfect. It pervaded great works of art like those of Michael Angelo and Shakespeare. Such as 'passeth the love of woman'. It was beautiful, it was pure, it was noble, it was intellectual – this love of an elder man with his experience of life, and the younger with all the joy and hope of life before him.

The witness made this speech with great emphasis and some signs of emotion, and there came from the gallery, at its conclusion, a medley of applause and hisses which his lordship at once ordered to be suppressed.

MR. GILL: I wish to call your attention to the style of your correspondence with Lord A. Douglas.

WITNESS: I am ready. I am never ashamed of the style of any of my writings.

MR. GILL: You are fortunate – or shall I say shameless? I refer to passages in two letters in particular.

WITNESS: Kindly quote them.

MR. GILL: In letter number one. You use this expression: 'Your slim gilt soul', and you refer to Lord Alfred's 'rose-leaf lips'.

WITNESS: The letter is really a sort of prose sonnet in answer to an acknowledgement of one I had received from Lord Alfred.

MR. GILL: Do you think that an ordinarily-constituted being would address such expressions to a younger man?

WITNESS: I am not, happily, I think, an ordinarily constituted being.

MR. GILL: It is agreeable to be able to agree with you, Mr. Wilde. [*Laughter.*]

WITNESS: There is, I assure you, nothing in either letter of which I need be ashamed.

From DE PROFUNDIS

In his essay *The Soul of Man under Socialism*, Wilde had argued against the ownership of private property. Now he had none. In Reading Gaol, he took stock of his life and wrote to Bosie the letter that has come to be known as *De Profundis*. It is a document unlike any other, a deep analysis, over some 50,000 words, of Wilde's own character, his past and present motives and his state of mind in the face of an uncertain future. It is also a call to Bosie. Pain, exasperation, affection, blame and sorrow still fanned the embers of Wilde's old, flawed love — but since the trial there had not been a word from Bosie, not even by letter. For Wilde, self-knowledge was the underlying aim in writing *De Profundis*. As for Bosie, it is possible that he may never have bothered to read it properly at all.

I must say to myself that neither you nor your father, multiplied a thousand times over, could possibly have ruined a man like me: that I ruined myself: and that nobody, great or small, can be ruined except by his own hand. [...] If I have brought this pitiless indictment against you, think what an indictment I bring without pity against myself. Terrible as what you did to me was, what I did to myself was far more terrible still.

I was a man who stood in symbolic relations to the art and culture of my age. I had realised this for myself at the very dawn of my manhood, and had forced my age to realise it afterwards. Few men hold such a position in their own lifetime and have it so acknowledged. It is usually discerned, if discerned at all, by the historian, or the critic, long after both the man and his age have passed away. With me it was different. I felt it myself, and made others feel it. Byron was a symbolic figure, but his relations were to the passion of his age and its weariness of passion. Mine were to something more noble, more permanent, of more vital issue, of larger scope.

The gods had given me almost everything. I had genius, a distinguished name, high social position, brilliancy, intellectual daring: I made art a philosophy and philosophy an art: I altered the minds of men and the colours of things: there was nothing I said or did that did not make people wonder: I took the drama, the most objective form known to art, and made it as personal a mode of expression as the lyric or the sonnet, at the same time that I widened its range and enriched its characterisation: drama, novel, poem in rhyme, poem in prose, subtle or fantastic dialogue, whatever I touched I made beautiful in a new mode of beauty: to truth itself I gave what is false no less than what is true as its rightful province, and showed that the false and the true are merely forms of intellectual existence. I treated Art as the supreme reality, and life as a mere mode of fiction. I awoke the imagination of my century so that it created myth and legend around me: I summed up all systems in a phrase and all existence in an epigram.

Along with these things, I had things that were different. I let myself be lured into long spells of senseless and sensual ease. I amused myself with being a *flâneur*, a dandy, a man of fashion. I surrounded myself with the smaller natures and the meaner minds. I became the spendthrift of my own genius, and to waste an eternal youth gave me a curious joy. Tired of being on the heights I deliberately went to the depths in the search for new sensations.

What the paradox was to me in the sphere of thought, perversity became to me in the sphere of passion. Desire, at the end, was a malady, or a madness, or both. I grew careless of the lives of others. I took pleasure where it pleased me and passed on. I forgot that every little action of the common day makes or unmakes character, and that therefore what one has done in the secret chamber one has some day to cry aloud on the housetops. I ceased to be Lord over myself. I was no longer the Captain of my Soul, and did not know it. I allowed you to dominate me, and your father to frighten me. I ended in horrible disgrace. There is only one thing for me now, absolute Humility: just as there is only one thing for you, absolute Humility also. You had better come down into the dust and learn it beside me.

I have lain in prison for nearly two years. Out of my nature has come wild despair; an abandonment to grief that was piteous even to look at: terrible and impotent rage: bitterness and scorn: anguish that wept aloud: misery that could find no voice: sorrow that was dumb. I have passed through every possible mood of suffering. Better than Wordsworth himself I know what Wordsworth meant when he said,

> Suffering is permanent, obscure, and dark
> And has the nature of Infinity.

But while there were times when I rejoiced in the idea that my sufferings were to be endless, I could not bear them to be without meaning. Now I find hidden away in my nature something that tells me that nothing in the whole world is meaningless, and suffering least of all.

That something hidden away in my nature, like a treasure in a field, is Humility.

It is the last thing left in me, and the best: the ultimate discovery at which I have arrived: the starting-point for a fresh development. It has come to me right out of myself, so I know that it has come at the proper time. It could not have come before, nor later. Had anyone told me of it, I would have rejected it. Had it been brought to me, I would have refused it. As I found it, I want to keep it. I must do so. It is the one thing that has in it the elements of life, of a new life, a *Vita Nuova* for me. Of all things it is the strangest. One cannot give it away, and another may not give it to one. One cannot acquire it, except by surrendering everything that one has. It is only when one has lost all things, that one knows that one possesses it.

Now that I realise that it is in me, I see quite clearly what I have got to do, what, in fact, I must do. And when I use such a phrase as that, I need not tell you that I am not alluding to any external sanction or command. I admit none. I am far more of an individualist than I ever was. Nothing seems to me of the smallest value except what one gets out of oneself. My nature is seeking a fresh mode of self-realisation. That is all I am concerned with. And the first thing that I have got to do is to free myself from any possible bitterness of feeling against you.

THE CRYSTAL OF A POET'S HEART

POEMS AND ENDINGS

C.3.3

From THE BALLAD OF READING GAOL

This extraordinary poem, the only substantial work Wilde completed after his release from prison, was first published under his prison number, 'C.3.3.' Wilde knew all too well what he was writing about. In Reading Gaol he became concerned about England's prison policy, and his letters to the newspapers helped to improve conditions a little. The ballad, which bears comparison with Coleridge's *The Rime of the Ancient Mariner*, has since become a favourite among those few who like to learn long poems by heart, though its hundred-plus stanzas pose a problem for anthologists under constraints of space. In 1936, W. B. Yeats shortened it for inclusion in *The Oxford Book of Modern Verse* and tried to make a virtue of necessity by claiming that he had 'plucked … its foreign feathers'. This selection takes a different view.

He did not wear his scarlet coat,
  For blood and wine are red,
And blood and wine were on his hands
  When they found him with the dead,
The poor dead woman whom he loved,
  And murdered in her bed.

He walked amongst the Trial Men
  In a suit of shabby grey;
A cricket cap was on his head,
  And his step seemed light and gay;
But I never saw a man who looked
  So wistfully at the day.

I never saw a man who looked
  With such a wistful eye
Upon that little tent of blue
  Which prisoners call the sky,
And at every drifting cloud that went
  With sails of silver by.

I walked, with other souls in pain,
  Within another ring,
And was wondering if the man had done
  A great or little thing,
When a voice behind me whispered low,
  'That fellow's got to swing.' […]

He did not wring his hands, as do
  Those witless men who dare
To try to rear the changeling Hope
  In the cave of black Despair:
He only looked upon the sun,
  And drank the morning air. [...]

And I and all the souls in pain,
  Who tramped the other ring,
Forgot if we ourselves had done
  A great or little thing,
And watched with gaze of dull amaze
  The man who had to swing. [...]

It is sweet to dance to violins
  When Love and Life are fair:
To dance to flutes, to dance to lutes
  Is delicate and rare:
But it is not sweet with nimble feet
  To dance upon the air! [...]

The Governor was strong upon
  The Regulations Act:
The Doctor said that Death was but
  A scientific fact:
And twice a day the Chaplain called
  And left a little tract.

And twice a day he smoked his pipe,
  And drank his quart of beer:
His soul was resolute, and held
  No hiding-place for fear;
He often said that he was glad
  The hangman's hands were near. […]

With slouch and swing around the ring
  We trod the Fool's Parade!
We did not care: we knew we were
  The Devil's Own Brigade:
And shaven head and feet of lead
  Make a merry masquerade.

We tore the tarry rope to shreds
  With blunt and bleeding nails;
We rubbed the doors, and scrubbed the floors,
  And cleaned the shining rails:
And, rank by rank, we soaped the plank,
  And clattered with the pails.

We sewed the sacks, we broke the stones,
  We turned the dusty drill:
We banged the tins, and bawled the hymns,
  And sweated on the mill:
But in the heart of every man
  Terror was lying still.

So still it lay that every day
  Crawled like a weed-clogged wave:
And we forgot the bitter lot
  That waits for fool and knave,
Till once, as we tramped in from work,
  We passed an open grave. [...]

At six o'clock we cleaned our cells,
  At seven all was still,
But the sough and swing of a mighty wing
  The prison seemed to fill,
For the Lord of Death with icy breath
  Had entered in to kill.

He did not pass in purple pomp,
  Nor ride a moon-white steed.
Three yards of cord and a sliding board
  Are all the gallows' need:
So with rope of shame the Herald came
  To do the secret deed. [...]

We waited for the stroke of eight:
  Each tongue was thick with thirst:
For the stroke of eight is the stroke of Fate
  That makes a man accursed,
And Fate will use a running noose
  For the best man and the worst. [...]

And as one sees most fearful things
  In the crystal of a dream,
We saw the greasy hempen rope
  Hooked to the blackened beam,
And heard the prayer the hangman's snare
  Strangled into a scream. [...]

There is no chapel on the day
  On which they hang a man:
The Chaplain's heart is far too sick,
  Or his face is far too wan,
Or there is that written in his eyes
  Which none should look upon.

So they kept us close till nigh on noon,
  And then they rang the bell,
And the warders with their jingling keys
  Opened each listening cell,
And down the iron stair we tramped,
  Each from his separate Hell.

Out into God's sweet air we went,
  But not in wonted way,
For this man's face was white with fear,
  And that man's face was grey,
And I never saw sad men who looked
  So wistfully at the day. [...]

Like ape or clown, in monstrous garb
  With crooked arrows starred,
Silently we went round and round
  The slippery asphalte yard;
Silently we went round and round,
  And no man spoke a word. [...]

For where a grave had opened wide,
  There was no grave at all:
Only a stretch of mud and sand
  By the hideous prison-wall,
And a little heap of burning lime,
  That the man should have his pall. [...]

They hanged him as a beast is hanged!
  They did not even toll
A requiem that might have brought
  Rest to his startled soul,
But hurriedly they took him out,
  And hid him in a hole. [...]

The Chaplain would not kneel to pray
  By his dishonored grave:
Nor mark it with that blessed Cross
  That Christ for sinners gave,
Because the man was one of those
  Whom Christ came down to save. [...]

I know not whether Laws be right,
  Or whether Laws be wrong;
All that we know who lie in gaol
  Is that the wall is strong;
And that each day is like a year,
  A year whose days are long. [...]

This too I know — and wise it were
  If each could know the same—
That every prison that men build
  Is built with bricks of shame,
And bound with bars lest Christ should see
  How men their brothers maim. [...]

And he of the swollen purple throat.
  And the stark and staring eyes,
Waits for the holy hands that took
  The Thief to Paradise;
And a broken and a contrite heart
  The Lord will not despise.

The man in red who reads the Law
  Gave him three weeks of life,
Three little weeks in which to heal
  His soul of his soul's strife,
And cleanse from every blot of blood
  The hand that held the knife.

And with tears of blood he cleansed the hand,
  The hand that held the steel:
For only blood can wipe out blood,
  And only tears can heal:
And the crimson stain that was of Cain
  Became Christ's snow-white seal. [...]

In Reading gaol by Reading town
  There is a pit of shame,
And in it lies a wretched man
  Eaten by teeth of flame,
In a burning winding-sheet he lies,
  And his grave has got no name. [...]

And all men kill the thing they love,
  By all let this be heard,
Some do it with a bitter look,
  Some with a flattering word,
The coward does it with a kiss,
  The brave man with a sword!

ON THE SALE BY AUCTION OF KEATS'S LOVE LETTERS

On the Continent, Wilde could write very little. He thought of composing 'a sort of companion to "The Ballad of Reading Gaol," in which I sing of liberty instead of prison, joy instead of sorrow, a kiss instead of an execution'. Nothing of it ever got written down: his heart was, as he said, a 'chamber of leaden echoes'.

He never saw his wife or his sons again. His health was uncertain, and not improved by heavy drinking. He had few friends, not much money, and almost no possessions. It was his beautiful books he missed most — sold off in batches by the bankruptcy auctioneer from a window of his family's Chelsea home.

But nobody could erase from the world his writings, and he knew that they were good. Just as the best-loved works of his beloved John Keats (the poet of 'Endymion') would endure for ever, so would the best-loved works of Oscar Wilde.

Years before, in 1885, he had sent this prophetic poem to a friend with the words, 'I wish I could grave my sonnets on an ivory tablet. Quill pens and notepaper are only good enough for bills of lading. A sonnet should always look well. Don't you think so?'

These are the letters which Endymion wrote
To one he loved in secret, and apart.
And now the brawlers of the auction mart
Bargain and bid for each poor blotted note,
Ay! for each separate pulse of passion quote
The merchant's price. I think they love not art
Who break the crystal of a poet's heart
That small and sickly eyes may glare and gloat.
Is it not said that many years ago,
In a far Eastern town, some soldiers ran
With torches through the midnight, and began
To wrangle for mean raiment, and to throw
Dice for the garments of a wretched man,
Not knowing the God's wonder, or His woe?

SOURCES

More than a century has passed since Oscar Wilde died, but though the first full, multi-volume scholarly edition of his complete writings has at last begun to appear (from Oxford University Press), it is not yet complete. Both before and after Wilde's death, his works were published with many variants. This book does not attempt to offer definitive versions but has drawn from whichever published source appeared to me as editor to offer the best text. Accordingly, the dates and details given below are those of each item's first appearance before the public. In many cases, Wilde (and other editors) would subsequently revise the listed items.

'The Picture of Dorian Gray: Preface', *Fortnightly Review*, March 1891.

'Hélas!' *Poems*, 1881.

'Requiescat', *Poems*, 1881.

'On Irish Home Rule', *St. Louis Globe-Democrat*, 27 February 1882.

'Impressions of America', lecture delivered Wandsworth Town Hall, 24 September 1883.

'To My Wife', in J.W.G. White (ed.), *Book-Song*, 1893.

'The Selfish Giant', in *The Happy Prince and Other Tales*, 1888.

'Aunt Jane's Ball', in W. Graham Robertson, *Time Was*, 1931.

'Impression du Matin', *The World*, March 1881.

'Lord Arthur Savile's Crime', *Court and Society Review*, May 1887.

'The Doer of Good', *Fortnightly Review*, July 1894.

'The Harlot's House', *Dramatic Review*, April 1885.

Salomé (Paris: Librairie de l'Art Indépendent), February 1893 (in French).

'A Few Maxims for the Instruction of the Over-Educated' (Anon.), *Saturday Review*, November 1894.

Lady Windermere's Fan, St James's Theatre, London, February 1892.

'The Soul of Man under Socialism', *Fortnightly*, February 1891.

A Woman of No Importance, Theatre Royal, London, April 1893.

The Importance of Being Earnest, St James's Theatre, London, February 1895.

The Trial of Oscar Wilde from the Shorthand Reports, privately published, Paris, 1906.

De Profundis, part published 1905; this version from *The Letters of Oscar Wilde*, edited by Rupert Hart-Davis, 1962.

The Ballad of Reading Gaol ('C.3.3.'), February 1898.

'On the Sale by Auction of Keats's Love Letters', *Dramatic Review*, January 1886.

ACKNOWLEDGEMENTS

I wish to thank the following for their kind help and good conversation on Wildean topics: Richard Miller, David Rose, Peter Thompson, Michael Warren and Thomas Wright. The dedication to this book is in memory of my great friend, Ruth Moller, whose lively interest in its progress can now, alas, be only imagined. Over many years she gave me so much.

DESIGNER'S NOTE

The visual art of the Aesthete was captured as a highly stylised patterned and symbolist form of natural art, at its height from about 1890 until 1910. Art Nouveau (New Art) was also the first major artistic movement where graphics played a key role. Accordingly, in this book, the visual breaks take their inspiration from both the literature and the artists of this period. Recurring themes here include complex patterns and symbols of flora, emulating the playing cards (and tarot cards) of the time.

ALL ART IS QUITE USELESS

The early days of the Aesthete. The patterns are a mixture of the Irish shamrock and the French *fleur-de-lis*, mirroring Huysmans *À Rebours*, an influential decadent work. The central peacock is a symbol of Victorian sexuality, while the two American eagles reflect Oscar's American trip.

A CHANGE IN THE WEATHER

Charles Robinson famously illustrated *The Happy Prince and Other Stories*. This is a patterned montage based on his work. The Christlike angel is a frequent presence in these stories and reflects Oscar's time as a young father and storyteller.

DISOBEDIENCE IS MAN'S ORIGINAL VIRTUE

Decadence and the Victorian attitude to sexuality are at loggerheads throughout Oscar's work. The patterned background is of a gingko leaf, a symbol of long life used throughout Art Nouveau. The foreground shows a dancing Salomé under an Eastern horseshoe arch. Lilies, another symbol of sexuality, are strewn at her feet.

IN FULL PURSUIT

Wilde is at the height of his fame with the huge success of the plays. The imagery is of the theatre, with a camelia, centre stage. Camelias were associated with homosexuality. The root vegetables are a reminder of the Marquis of Queensberry's sardonic gift of a bouquet of vegetables.

THE LOVE THAT DARE NOT SPEAK ITS NAME

The Green Carnation, a symbol of Wilde himself, reputedly first worn by an actress on the opening night of *Lady Windermere's Fan*. It is worshipped by two sphinxes, against a background of knotted undergrowth. A period of turmoil.

THE CRYSTAL OF A POET'S HEART

The centrepiece is 'C.3.3.' Wilde's number when in Reading Gaol, with a singing bird trapped in a beautiful cage. The black roses in a cruciform shape symbolise his death.